I don't set trends. I just find out what they are and I exploit them.

—Dick Clark
American disc jockey and
music-industry executive

Household
GOLD™

Dr. Steve W. Price

Household Gold™

by Dr. Steve W. Price
Copyright 2003 by Steve W. Price

Trademarked by INTI Publishing, Inc., 2003

Household Gold™
Household Goldmine™
Anyway Money™
Stealth Wealth™
Retail Estate™

Printed in United States of America
First edition December 2003

ISBN: 1-891279-13-0
Published by INTI Publishing
intipublishing.com
Tampa, FL

Cover design and text layout by Parry Design Studio

Dedication

*For my mother, Mary Evelyn Price,
the best mom any kid ever had.*

Acknowledgment

It's only fitting that a book about Household Gold should pay tribute to Workplace Gold, that is, the people who make my going to work every morning a joy instead of a job.

Thank you Katherine Glover, president of INTI Publishing, for leading our team with determination in your heart and a smile on your face.

Thank you Burke Hedges, mentor and business partner, for seeing talents in me before I saw them in myself.

Thank you Sandee Lorenzen, our operations director, for never failing to lift my spirits with the song in your voice.

Thank you Gail Brown, our accountant, for wearing at least five other hats on top of your accounting visor.

Thank you Julia Bullough, our shipping manager, for organizing a warehouse that has quadrupled in size in two years.

And thank you Debbie Cortes, our marketing director and the newest member of our team, for your calm, professional manner and ever-positive attitude.

Thanks to all of you, I have more fun at work than most people have on weekends. From the bottom of my heart, I say to each of you, "Thank you for being you. I wouldn't want you any other way."

Table of Contents

Trademarks of INTI Publishing*

Household Gold™

Household Goldmine™

Anyway Money™

Retail Estate™

Stealth Wealth™

*The above phrases are trademarks of INTI Publishing, Inc., and must not be used in print, audio, video, electronically, or digitly via CDs, DVDs, or the Internet, without written permission from INTI Publishing, Inc.

Introduction

It's obvious to everyone that owning a house beats renting because owning builds equity.

Well, just as houses contain equity, households contain equity, too. Yet nobody thinks about owning their own households!

Introduction

Household Equity:
A Goldmine That
Never Runs Dry

*The thoughts that come to us unsought,
and, as it were, drop into the mind, are
commonly the most valuable.*

—John Locke
philosopher

Y ou've likely never heard the expression "Anyway Money™"

And for good reason—I made it up.

Anyway Money is the money you're spending to maintain your household and lifestyle. Since you have to spend this money *anyway,* it only makes sense to position yourself to create *some income*—instead of *all outgo*—on those necessary expenditures, wouldn't you agree?

Just think about the dozens, if not hundreds, of products and services that you have to buy on a regular basis.

You have to buy detergent and cleaning supplies, *anyway*.

You have to buy makeup and beauty products, *anyway*.

You have to buy vitamins and supplements, *anyway*.

You have to buy scores of household services including Internet, wireless, and long distance phone services, *anyway*.

So, since you and millions of other hard-working people have to take money OUT of your households to buy these things *anyway*... wouldn't it be great if a percentage of that money could be channeled back INTO your household?

Sure it would!

Well, that's why I wrote this book—to teach you the proven strategies that will enable you to convert household expenses into Household Gold™!

Not Just Cash Back, but Cash Flow!

The strategies you're about to learn are similar to the TV commercial for Discover Card that says, "Why not get paid for the things you buy *anyway*?"

Why not, indeed?

But Household Gold begins where Discover Card ends! By leveraging the Household Gold concept, you not only get *cash back* on your purchases, you can also position yourself to earn *cash flow* from the products and services other households purchase, while saving yourself thousands of dollars a year in taxes. In fact, Household Gold has the potential to become a *cash cow* for you once you learn and apply the principles in this book!

The beauty of Household Gold is its simplicity—it empowers you to create wealth from the purchases you and everyone else makes *anyway*... while, at the same time, it empowers you to own your own life. Since everybody would like to make more money and call their own shots, *anyway*, why not learn how to do both?

My Introduction to Anyway Money

The concept of Anyway Money was years in the making—30 years to be exact! Here's my story of how I was first introduced to Anyway Money.

In 1974, when I was 28 years old and renting an apartment, I decided it was time to buy a house. I'd been renting since graduating from college, and I got tired of paying rent and not having anything to show for it. So, I bought a small, two-bedroom "handyman special" (which is real estate jargon for a dump) on a quiet, tree-lined street for $15,000, which was bottom-of-the-barrel cheap even by 1970s standards.

Working nights and weekends, I renovated the place and sold it a year later for $28,500. A month later, I used the profits to buy a bigger house in a nicer neighborhood.

Unbeknownst to me at the time, this was my first foray into Anyway Money. Since I had to have a place to live *anyway...* and since my rent money and my mortgage payment cost the same amount of money *anyway,* it only made sense to own my own house and build equity rather than continuing to rent so that my landlord could increase *his* equity.

My first experience owning real estate was so positive that it led me to become not just a homeowner, but also a real estate investor. Today I own three apartment buildings and three condominiums worth several million dollars, and I'm always on the lookout for great deals.

The advantages of owning rental properties are enormous. Investment properties build equity and appreciation... they're inflation proof... they offer great tax deductions... and once the mortgages are retired, they kick off residual income year in and year out.

Yep, owning real estate is a great investment. Statistics show that 70% of multi-millionaires made their money in real estate. But unlike buying a home, which can be purchased by Anyway Money (you've got to spend money on housing *anyway,* so it's better to own than rent), investment properties require Additional Money.

Additional Money is the money that you have to spend above and beyond the money it takes to maintain your household. For example, if you buy a used car for your son or daughter, that takes Additional Money. If you invest in the stock market or in real estate, that takes Additional Money. Mortgage companies typically require 20% down for investment properties, which means to buy a $100,000 rental house, you'd have to come out of pocket $20,000, not to mention money for renovation costs and emergency repairs. For 99% of the population, $20,000 is serious, Additional Money.

Yes, owning real estate can be a terrific wealth-creating opportunity, but it's not for everyone. It takes a big chunk of Additional Money to buy and maintain rental properties. And let's face it, these days Additional Money is a rare commodity in most households.

How I Discovered That Households Have Equity, too

One afternoon in December of 2002, I was in my office pulling together the records for my annual meeting with my accountant. I was rummaging through my real estate records when I came across a folder labeled, "Mom and Dad's Estate." Both my parents had passed away in the early 1990s, and as sole executor, it was my job to liquidate their estate. As I thumbed through the papers, two documents jumped out at me.

The first document was the closing statement for the sale of their home, which sold for $40,000. The second document was the final accounting from the auctioneer who sold all of the stuff *inside* my parent's house—furniture, clothing, jewelry, etc. The final estate sale totaled just over $10,000. As I compared the two documents side by side—$40,000 proceeds for the house, $10,000 for the household—I was suddenly struck by an obvious insight:

Not only do houses have equity, *households have equity as well!*

I remember thinking to myself, "It's obvious to everyone that owning a house beats renting because owning builds equity. Well, just as houses contain equity, households contain equity, too. *Yet nobody thinks about owning their own households!*"

Think about it—people spend hundreds of dollars, if not thousands of dollars, a month maintaining their households. Which means that millions of people are letting trillions of dollars slip though their fingers every year without tapping into any of the equity. What a waste! Every household in the world is sitting on a goldmine of Anyway Money, and they don't even realize it!

Household Equity: A Goldmine That Never Runs Dry

There's a simple way to calculate how much equity you have in your household. All you have to do is look at your homeowner's insurance policy to see how much the personal property INSIDE your home is insured for.

When I checked my homeowner's policy, I was surprised to learn that the contents of my house were insured for $97,000, which is how much my insurer estimates it would cost to replace the durable goods in my home, such as furniture, clothing, bedding, artwork, etc.

But in truth, my household equity far exceeds $97,000 because I have to replenish the consumables in my household on a regular basis... PLUS I'm always updating or adding to the stuff in my household. For example, last month I bought a computer for my daughter's room, replaced the old VCR with a combination DVD/VCR player, and replaced my bedroom blinds with floor-to-ceiling drapes.

Over the course of a year, I *easily spend* between $500 to $1,000 A MONTH on my household essentials. Households with three or four children might spend two, even three times that amount each month.

That's why I say household equity is a goldmine that never runs dry. Every time a product or service in your household has to be replenished, replaced, added or updated, you're adding more equity to your household, isn't that true?

See the Obvious

Unfortunately, if you're like most people, *you're spending money* to acquire more equity, but *you're not making any money* on that newly acquired equity. The good news is that you've got a household goldmine of equity that never runs dry. But the bad news is you're allowing someone else to mine that equity instead of you! If you haven't positioned yourself to profit from the millions of households that are spending trillions of dollars each year on household equity, then you're overlooking an obvious opportunity.

See the obvious, folks. SEE THE OBVIOUS!

Look, it's obvious to people that owning a home beats renting, which is why almost 70% of Americans own their own homes. But it's equally obvious that households have equity, too, just as houses do. Yet very few people position themselves to take advantage of mining the equity in millions of households all over the world. What a lost opportunity—and what a shame!

Think about it—just as you have to spend money on either rent or a mortgage *anyway,* you also have to spend money on household essentials *anyway.* So, wouldn't it be great if you could benefit from the equity of those household products and services, just as you benefit from owning your own home? Of course.

That's why I wrote *Household Gold*—to shine a light on an obvious source of wealth that the vast majority of people have been overlooking. My goal is to turn an *obvious oversight* into a *profound insight* about a powerful wealth-building concept that is literally right in front of your nose.

Household Gold: The Anyway Money Recovery Program

Today, Anyway Money is more important than ever—it's a way for average people to take control of their lives again, to reach up and grab that gold ring known the world over as The American Dream.

Thanks to the Household Gold concept, hard-working people can position themselves to earn anywhere from part-time income to a full-time fortune... PLUS they can own their own lives and control their own destinies in the process.

By applying the simple yet powerful strategies in this book, you, too, can take control of your finances... take control of your future... and take control of your life.

So, how much Anyway Money would you like to earn, anyway? A couple thousand a year? Ten thousand? A hundred thousand? More? No matter what your financial dreams and goals, the Household Gold concept can be leveraged to accomplish them. Millions of people all over the world are doing just that.

Why not you?

After all, it's your household, *anyway.*

You have to maintain your household, *anyway.*

So, since you're spending the money *anyway,* the next step is obvious—start turning your household expenses... into Household Gold!

Part 1

Staking Your Claim to Household Gold™

Successful people see the obvious. Successful people go after the sure thing, rather than chasing after the pie-in-the-sky, get-rich-quick deals, such as gambling.

Chapter 1

Thar's Gold on Them There Shelves!

Like the gold-greedy 49-ers, less than 1% of the population strikes it rich in a casino or a courtroom.

But 100% of the population spends hundreds or even thousands of dollars a month on household essentials, creating a tremendous opportunity for people with the vision to see the obvious.

1

Thar's Gold on Them There Shelves!

"Quick and easy" is seldom quick and never easy.

—Mark Twain

"**I** have found it," announced James Marshall to the workers building a sawmill near Sacramento, California, on a clear November day in 1847.

"What is 'it?'" asked a perplexed laborer named William Scott.

"Gold," replied Marshall.

"Oh, that can't be," said Scott.

"I know it to be nothing else," replied Marshall.

Who could have guessed that this calm conversation between a handful of hard scrabble, poorly educated men struggling to survive in a sparsely populated territory 2,000 miles west of St. Louis, the western-most outpost of American civilization, would be the seed that sprouted the California

Gold Rush, the greatest land migration of humans since the Crusades in the Middle Ages?

Lured by visions of easy riches, thousands of hopefuls spilled into the San Francisco area each week. They came on horseback. On sailing ships. On steam ships. On horse-drawn wagons. On ox-drawn carts. On mules. And, as last resort, on foot.

By 1853, more than a quarter of a million people had migrated to San Francisco as Gold Fever swept across the globe like a wind-blown virus. Tent cities sprung up overnight. And within months, the small, little-known port city of San Francisco exploded into a bustling, world-famous boom town.

California or Bust!

How contagious was Gold Fever? Hours after printing the front-page headline, "GOLD! GOLD! GOLD!," a San Francisco newspaper was forced to close when the entire staff ran off to the gold fields. Within weeks of the discovery of gold, store owners had to pay employees quadruple their normal wages to keep them from running off. And the waters of San Francisco Bay became nearly unnavigable as hundreds of ships bobbed unattended after entire crews jumped ship to search for gold.

The rumors about the discovery of gold proved to be true, although the stories of easy riches turned out to be greatly exaggerated. Truth be told, only a few thousand of the 250,000 prospectors were lucky enough to uncover $50 to $500 a day in gold nuggets from the river beds scattered across Sacramento Valley.

But for every lucky miner who struck it rich, 100 unlucky miners died from contagious diseases that ravaged the unsanitary mining camps. For every lucky miner who accumulated enough gold to grubstake a business or a ranch, 1,000 unlucky miners lost their windfalls in rigged card games or blew it on rotgut whiskey purchased at inflated prices.

When the Gold Rush dust settled, the vast majority of the prospectors walked away from their claims with nothing more than bad backs and blistered hands. Sadly, for most of the miners, "California or Bust" turned into "Busted in California."

Retailers Were the Real Winners of the Gold Rush

Most of the miners came up empty handed in their rush to get rich, but the same can't be said for the merchants who sold them goods and services—*the retailers made money hand over fist!*

Sam Brannon was the first businessman to recognize that there was more money to be made in supplying miners than there was in sifting through thousands of pounds of gravel and silt to find an ounce of gold. Brannon owned a general store in Sacramento. When word got out that gold had been discovered, Brannon bought a pouch of gold dust and headed to San Francisco, where he strutted up and down the busiest streets waving the gold over his head and shouting, "Gold discovered just outside Sacramento!"

Within days, hundreds of men descended on Brannon's store to buy prospecting supplies: picks, shovels, pots, pans, clothing, tents, bedding, candles, coffee, boots, soap, and so on. It didn't take long for Brannon's store to far outperform all but a few of the tens of thousands of small claims dotting Sacramento Valley. During the boom years, Brannon's General Merchandise Store was moving $5,000 worth of merchandise *a day* (the equivalent of at least $50,000 these days), prompting a fellow Sacramento businessman to remark, "Brannon possesses one of the surest fortunes in California. He has what everyone needs and charges what the market will bear."

See the Obvious

What lesson can we learn from one rich retailer and the hundreds of thousands of busted forty-niners? Simply this. *Successful people see the obvious.* Successful people go after the sure thing, rather than chasing after the pie-in-the-sky, get-rich-quick deals, such as gold mining and gambling.

During the Gold Rush, it was obvious to Sam Brannon and the other retailers that the real goldmine wasn't to be found in the hills and riverbeds around Sacramento but in the businesses that supplied what the miners' needed. Because they took advantage of the obvious, Brannon and his buddies got richer than they ever dreamed possible.

The same holds true today as it did during the California Gold Rush—*successful people see the obvious* and position themselves to profit from it. In 1849, even the miners understood that very few of them would strike it rich. But it was obvious that 100% of the miners would need to buy household essentials to set up their claims. So, why did so many people chase after the one-in-a-million, get-rick-quick opportunity when a 100%-guaranteed opportunity was right under their noses? Because the golden glare of a get-rich-quick opportunity blinded them to the obvious.

Today, the get-rich-quick opportunity isn't the gold fields of California but something I call the "Three Ls"—Las Vegas, the lottery, and lawsuits. As you will learn in the next chapter, more and more people are trying to strike it rich with the Three Ls. But, like the 49-ers, less than 1% of the population strikes it rich in a casino or a courtroom, but 100% of the population spends hundreds or even thousands of dollars a month on household essentials, creating a tremendous opportunity for people with the vision to see the obvious.

Right Under Your Nose

Have you heard the joke about the two blondes standing on opposite banks of a river? The first blonde shouts to the other, *"Yoo-hoo! How can I get to the other side?"* The second blonde looks up and down the river, scratches her head, and then shouts back, *"But you ARE on the other side!"*

That's the way I feel when I try to explain the Household Gold concept—people don't have to travel to the other side of the river to mine gold. They already ARE on the other side, and the gold is right under their noses... right at their fingertips. All they have to do is open their eyes and see the obvious—their household is packed with gold nuggets just waiting to be mined.

The concept behind household gold reminds me of Russell Conwell's oft-told story, "Acres of Diamonds." The allegedly true story goes like this: A poor farmer in Africa spends his life traveling all over the continent looking for diamonds. He returns home a broken man and dies without ever finding a single diamond.

When a minister drops by to give comfort to the farmer's family, he spies a large crystalline rock sitting on the fireplace mantle. He asks where the rock came from, and the widow tells him the farm is littered with these odd-looking rocks. The minister then informs her that this odd-looking rock is a diamond, which means her family must be sitting on "acres of diamonds."

Likewise, when you're inside your house, you're sitting on acres of gold—Household Gold. Unfortunately, most people are like the farmer in Africa—they think the only way to strike it rich is to travel to some glamorous place and gamble (like Las Vegas) or travel to the local convenience store and participate in a one-in-a-zillion game of chance (like the lottery).

Before I show you how to mine your Household Gold, I'd like to take a moment to explain why the get-rich-quick-with-one-big-score mentality that began 150 years ago with the California Gold Rush is alive and well today… and why it's sidetracking hundreds of thousands of people every year from realizing their dreams.

Let's turn the page to the next chapter to discover why I say that the "big score" Gold Rush mentality so prevalent today is the fool's gold of the 21st century.

Chapter 2

Are You Rolling the Dice For The American Dream?

What the 49-ers did was to pass along a legacy of luck to the world. Unfortunately, that legacy hasn't died out over the last 150 years. It's only gotten stronger.

As a result, today tens of millions of people who should know better are rolling the dice for the American Dream with the Three Ls—Las Vegas, the lottery, and lawsuits.

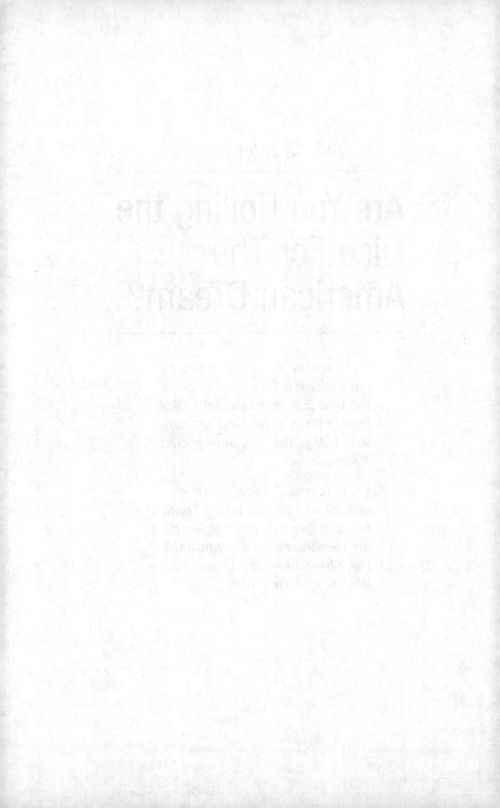

2

Are You Rolling the Dice For The American Dream?

I lost $10,000 at the horse races one afternoon, and I spent 10 years and a million dollars trying to win it back.

—Mickey Rooney,
actor

In the long, loud explosion of history, the California Gold Rush was a firecracker, lasting five years from start to finish. Yet, amazingly, the echo of those boom years hasn't faded with time but continues to grow louder with each passing generation.

Why?

Ironically, the lasting impact of the Gold Rush wasn't on the economy but on the culture, for, like a miner's pickax shattering slate, *the Gold Rush shattered the prevailing paradigm of wealth creation.*

You see, pre-Gold Rush, people believed it took a lifetime of hard work to create wealth. And they were right—it took years of back-breaking work to build a prosperous farm or ranch. But post-Gold Rush, people began to believe wealth could be created in a golden moment of good fortune, instead of long years of labor.

In the fascinating book, *The Age of Gold: The California Gold Rush and the New American Dream,* historian H. W. Brands theorizes that the Gold Rush was one of those rare, seminal events in history that trigger a seismic shift in how ordinary people view their world:

> "The Gold Rush changed the way Americans viewed their destinies. Striking it rich quickly transformed the traditional Puritan ethic of hard work and the gradual accumulation of wealth. In the aftermath of the Gold Rush, a New American Dream was born—the enduring conviction that sudden wealth was potentially within everyone's grasp and that boldness and luck were at least as important as steadfastness and frugality."

Passing Along a Legacy of Luck

H.W. Brands observation is right on the mark—the Gold Rush forever changed people's notions about what it took to get their slice of the American Dream pie. Only a few miners struck it rich. But the tidal wave of publicity surrounding the rare miner who hit pay dirt flooded across the country, washing away people's common sense while watering their greed. Thus, the Gold Rush forced open the door for the get-rich-quick mentality to enter the American consciousness.

What the 49-ers did was to pass along a legacy of luck to the world. Unfortunately, that legacy hasn't died out over the last 150 years. It's only gotten stronger. As a result, today tens of millions of people who should know better are rolling the dice for the American Dream with the Three Ls—Las Vegas, the lottery, and lawsuits.

Folks, don't make the mistake the 49-ers made, or you're going to end up like the vast majority of the 49-ers ended up—desperate… disappointed… and dead broke! You see, the 49-ers bought into the get-rich-quick plan—and most ended up busted. But the retailers bought into the smart-and-steady plan—and they ended up rich.

Yes, somebody has to win the lottery. But odds are, it isn't going to be you. So stop deluding yourself. Stop throwing your money away on what I call the "no-work New American Dream." And instead, start doing what it takes to achieve the *true* American Dream—start looking for real, proven opportunities, just like the Gold Rush-era retailers did.

The True American Dream vs. the New American Dream

Now, before I start our discussion on the no-work New American Dream, let me clarify what the true American Dream is all about. When I talk about the American Dream, I'm not limiting it to the geographical boundaries of the United States of America. Over the last century, the American Dream has been exported to every free country in the world.

Yes, the American Dream was birthed by the American Revolution and nurtured by free enterprise. But for the last 200-plus years, the American Dream has been adopted by every continent on earth and has touched the hearts of billions of people so that today, the American Dream can truly be called the world-wide American Dream. Wherever free people and free markets exist, you'll find people striving for their version of the true American Dream.

So the question becomes, "How do people capture the American Dream?" Before the Gold Rush, everyone agreed that the only way to achieve the American Dream was to earn it "the old-fashioned way," through hard work, discipline, sacrifice, and perseverance. Yes, many people are still using these time-tested values in pursuit of their American Dream.

Unfortunately, the Gold Rush ushered in a get-rich-quick paradigm that is rapidly replacing the old character-based approach to success. And worst of all, the entity that is most responsible for pumping up the new, no-work paradigm is the U.S. government!

The Government Greases the Slippery Slope

The underpinnings of the no-work New American Dream are the "Three Ls"—Las Vegas, the lottery, and lawsuits. Each of the Three Ls is a slacker's paradise—huge returns without doing any work. The sad part is, the Three Ls are growing like bamboo in a tropical rain forest—and the government is the gardener!

In the 1970s, gambling was banned in all 50 states except Nevada and New Jersey. Today gambling is legal in 28 states, generates $63 billion a year, and is spreading like wildfire across the nation. Conveniently ignoring the bankruptcies, broken homes, and other social ills that gambling leaves in its wake, dozens of revenue-hungry states are encouraging American Indian tribes to open casinos (rather than developing real economies) so that the states can pocket the tax money.

As I write this, there are 87 Native American gaming enterprises operating in 23 states, employing tens of thousands of workers, and generating almost $10 billion in annual revenue. *Today, casinos on Indian reservations create more revenues than Las Vegas and Atlantic City combined!*

Thanks to our short-sighted politicians, legalized gambling is THE major growth industry in the U.S. Today 90% of U.S. households live within two hours' drive of a casino, enabling 25% of adults over age 21 to visit a casino in 2000. In 2001, Americans spent a record $25 BILLION in casinos.

Yep, gambling is big business. And getting bigger.

When you add the $25 billion spent gambling in casinos to the $38 billion spent on lottery tickets in 2001, you come up with *$63 billion spent on gambling IN ONE YEAR!*

That's A LOT of moolah, folks! Compare what Americans spent on gambling in 2001 to some other major household expenses:

Sample Household Expenditures in 2001

Expenditure	Total Money Spent
Gambling (lotteries & Casinos)	**$63 billion**
Computer hardware, software, etc.	$55 billion
Furniture & bedding	$48 billion
Sporting goods	$35 billion
Kitchenware & home furnishings	$32 billion
TVs, VCRs, DVDs, & Video Cams	$20 billion

It's pretty amazing to think that Americans spent more on gambling than they did on computers and three times more on gambling than on TVs, VCRs, and DVD players, isn't it? But it's true. And it's only going to get worse, as more and more people jump aboard the no-work New American Dream train.

Lawsuits: The Lottery in a Three-Piece Suit

Lotteries and Las Vegas are growing in popularity, but they pale in comparison to their older brother, lawsuits! According to Lord Levene, chairman of Lloyd's of London Insurance, the cost of the American tort system has increased 100-fold in the last 50 years, quickly approaching $300 billion a year. He goes on to say that the cost of litigation in the U.S, is the equivalent of a 5% tax on every working person's wages.

"Litigation causes an unbelievable drain on the U.S. economy," Levene says, "because insurers have no choice but to pass on the cost to consumers through higher premiums."

You have to laugh at the absurdity of people who actually believe they've got a chance to overcome one-in-a-zillion odds to win the lottery. But the hands-down winners of the no-work New American Dream Biggest Belly Laughs Contest are frivolous lawsuits.

Listed below are my four favorite laughable lawsuits filed in 2001:

- A California man is suing the local library for $1.5 million because he suffered "significant, lasting, extreme, and severe mental anguish and emotional distress" after the 10-pound library cat attacked his 50-pound Labrador Retriever.
- Four overweight teenage girls from the Bronx in New York sued McDonald's for causing their obesity and health problems, arguing that McDonald's deceived customers about the dangers of its products and failed to display nutritional information prominently enough.
- An Illinois woman sued McDonald's, Wal-Mart, a cup manufacturer, and *her own* mother after a cup of hot coffee from McDonald's burned her ankle when the cup fell out of her Wal-Mart cup holder in her mother's car.

• A Florida man sued six taverns and liquor stores plus the electric company because he suffered burns while grabbing power lines during his drunken climb up an electrical tower. The intoxicated man had to climb over a fence and a locked gate to reach the power lines.

The only thing more laughable than these goofy lawsuits are the attorneys who agree to take them. Why would people file such laughable lawsuits? One reason and one reason only—*sometimes they win!* What's worse, jury awards are on the increase! No wonder New York City budgets $30 million a year to settle lawsuits stemming from accidents on city property and sidewalks.

Stop Gambling with Your Dreams

Folks, are you beginning to see how the Gold Rush set the stage for the shift away from the smart-and-steady paradigm of wealth creation to the get-rich-quick-and-easy paradigm? Whether it's lawsuits... legalized gambling... or lotteries, millions of people the world over are rolling the dice on their American Dream.

News flash!—there's no need to gamble away your dreams! Why leave your home in search of gold when you're sitting on a goldmine right in your own home? I mean, see the obvious, people.

See the obvious!

It was obvious to the retailers during the California Gold Rush that mining for gold was a high risk proposition—a gamble, if you will. And it was equally obvious to the retailers that distributing household essentials to a growing population was a low-risk, high return opportunity that only comes around once in a lifetime. So, they opted for retailing household essentials over gambling in the gold fields—and they got rich for seeing the obvious.

Same goes for today. It's obvious that when it comes to gambling, there are very few winners and LOTS of losers. It's obvious that the only people consistently making money in Las Vegas and the lotteries are the casino owners and the state treasuries.

So, see the obvious!

It's obvious that you (and everyone else) must spend hundreds if not thousands of dollars a month to maintain your household.

It's obvious that households contain equity, just as houses do.

It's obvious that it's smarter and less risky to build a business on Anyway Money than having to spend lots of Additional Money.

And it's obvious that since you and everyone else has to buy household products and services on a regular basis *anyway,* it just makes sense to keep some of that Anyway Money in your household where it belongs.

What could be more obvious than that?

When you finally see the obvious, what you'll see is that your household is littered with gold nuggets just waiting to be mined. So, let's turn the page to find out what those veins of gold in your household are really worth.

Chapter 3

Stealth Wealth™: Discovering the Gold Hidden in Your Household

The American economy totals somewhere around $10 trillion a year. The 118 million households in America spend $1.1 trillion each year on household products and services. Which means that more than 10% of America's $10 trillion-a-year economy is being spent on Household Gold.

3

Stealth Wealth™: Discovering the Gold Hidden in Your Household

Wealth is not the same as income. If you make a good income each year and spend it all, you're not getting wealthier. You're just living high. Wealth is what you accumulate, not what you spend.

Thomas J. Stanley & William D. Danko
authors of "The Millionaire Next Door"

S ee if you can solve this riddle.

What's as big as a house... flies like a bird... but is invisible? Give up?

The answer is a military aircraft called the Stealth bomber.

Originally named the B2 bomber, the Stealth earned its nickname because it can't be detected by enemy radar. The

Stealth bomber's irregular-shaped surfaces are designed to deflect radio waves into space, instead of back to a radar dish. As a result, even though the Stealth bomber is the size of a house, it's invisible to radar.

Now, see if you can solve a riddle similar to the one above.

What fills up a house... is worth tens of thousands of dollars... but is invisible?

The answer is stealth wealth™.

The value of people's Retail Estate™—that is, all the stuff inside a house bought from retail stores—is like the Stealth bomber. Retail Estate is as big as a house, but it's "invisible" to most people because it doesn't register on their mental radar. As a result, even though people LOOK at their household possessions every single day, they don't SEE the wealth hidden in those possessions.

That's why I call Retail Estate "stealth wealth." It's real. It's huge. But people can't see it with their out-dated mental radar. And if they don't see the wealth in the products surrounding them, they can't take advantage of their hidden value, can they?

To Improve Your Finances, Improve Your Mental Radar

Yogi Berra, the hall-of-fame baseball player who is famous for his seemingly nonsensical sayings, said, "You can see a lot just by looking."

Ironically, Yogi is right—you have to *look* before you can *see.* But before you can really *see,* you have to update your outdated mental radar by opening your mind to new ways of seeing the same old objects. Once you replace your old mental radar with updated, stealth-wealth-detecting radar, then you will immediately *see* that every room in your house is littered with Household Gold.

To illustrate what I mean, let's *look* inside the smallest room of your house—your laundry room—to *see* the stealth wealth that you're walking by every single day. Follow me as I open the door to your laundry room to identify a few of the Household Gold products sitting on your cabinet shelves: laundry detergent... pre-soak detergent... fabric softener sheets... fabric softener liquid... bleach... stain remover... spray starch... multi-purpose cleaner... and spray bottles.

That pretty much covers the basics in my laundry room. What about yours? Now let's take a moment to see the *potential dollar value* of the Retail Estate in this one small room of your house.

Let's start with laundry detergent, the mainstay of every laundry room. According to the Soap and Detergent Association (SDA), the average household washes almost 10 loads of laundry each week at an average cost of 25 cents per load for detergent. That calculates to $2.50 per week, or $10 a month for detergent.

How a Small Load of Laundry Can Turn into a Big Load of Money

Now, at first glance, $120 a year spent on laundry detergent doesn't seem like much money. *But this is just one product in just one household!* When you total up all of the households in America, that $10 per month per household to do the laundry adds up to *Americans spending $5 BILLION A YEAR—just on laundry detergent!*

Let this figure of $5 billion sink in a bit. A billion is a thousand million. Which means Americans (who make

up only 6% of the world's population) are spending five...
thousand... million... dollars... each... and... every... year on
one single household product!

Let's take it one step further. The average laundry room
contains eight different products, all of which need to be
replenished on a regular basis. According to the SDA,
Americans spend another $6 billion on bleach, pretreatments,
fabric softener, and starch. No wonder that Proctor &
Gamble, the world's biggest household and personal products
manufacturer, sells $42 billion worth of household essentials
every year (and worldwide sales are showing no sign of
slowing down).

Now are you beginning to see the sparkle of the gold in
your household?

Let's Take the Stealth-Wealth Tour

Let's take a moment to tour your house room by room so
that you can see the stealth wealth sitting on your floors and
tucked away in your closets and drawers. Let's start our tour
with the two biggest rooms, the living room and dining room.

Living and Dining Rooms

Stand in the middle of your living room and turn slowly
in a circle. What do you see? Furniture... TV... VCR and
DVD... stereo system... shelving... drapes... tables... table
cloths... chairs... rugs... vases... baskets... bowls... candles...
telephones... crystal... lamps... clocks... and photo frames
and albums.

How about the dining room—what do you see there?
Dining room table... chairs... candle holders... buffet...
lighting... and wall treatments. Now let's move on to the
bedrooms.

Bedrooms

Just look at all the stuff in your bedrooms that you bought at retail from stores: beds... mattresses... mattress pads... end tables... sheets... dressers... pillows... blankets... mirrors... bookcases... scented candles... and a TV (the average American household owns three TVs).

Open the closet doors, and you'll see even more stealth wealth: dresses... skirts... purses... women's' shoes... men's shoes... running shoes... boots... slippers... sports coats... pants... and spare wooden hangers.

Don't forget to open the jewelry box: watches... rings... earrings... bracelets... broaches... and necklaces.

Bathrooms

Now, we're off to the bathroom. Just look at all the household items in the medicine cabinet: vitamins... nutritional supplements... weight loss products... pain relievers... magnetic therapy products... and energy boosters. What about the stuff sitting on the countertop? soap... hair spray... combs... toothpaste... tooth brushes... deodorant... aftershave... cologne... razors... shaving cream... shampoo... and styling mousse.

Now it's time to open the drawers: lipstick... blush... foundation... moisturizer... body lotion.. cleanser... mascara... eye shadow... nail polish... night cream... bubble bath... and sun screen.

Oh, mustn't forget to look under the sink: toilet paper... cleaning supplies... mouthwash... curling iron... and hair dryer.

Kitchen

Where do we start in the kitchen? How about the pantry? meal replacement bars... snacks... cereal... storage containers... mops and brooms... canned food... pots and pans... and pet food. In the kitchen cabinets we see dishes... bowls...glasses... cups... silverware... mixers... cookie sheets... roasting pans... and a food processor.

On the countertop sit a toaster... coffee maker... blender... and cutlery block set. Can't overlook those major kitchen appliances: refrigerator... stove... microwave... dish washer... plus, the garbage disposal and water filter.

Oops—almost forgot to check under the sink: dish washing liquid... automatic dishwasher soap... all-purpose cleaner... hand soap... rubber gloves... floor cleaner... window cleaner... and room deodorizer.

Garage

While we're at it, might as well peek in the garage. We see oil... gas additive... garage door opener... tools... car mats... car wash and wax... interior cleaner... tar remover... and vinyl protector.

I've listed more than 100 products just off the top of my head—and that doesn't include household and personal services, such as long-distance telephone service... wireless service... Internet service provider... home security system... credit card services... even travel services and insurance, just to name a few. It's amazing how much stealth wealth one household can accumulate over time, isn't it?

When you add up everything in your household, how much do you think you paid for all of the products and services contained in your household? $5,000? $10,000?

$25,000? Or more? To answer that question, consider these statistics for the average American household:

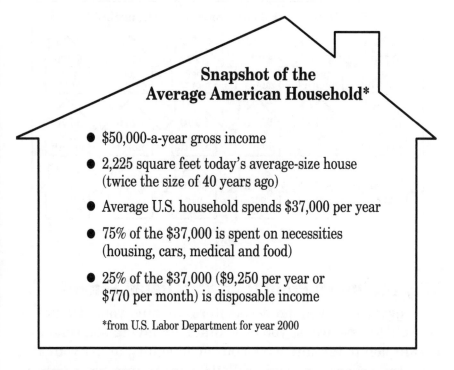

Snapshot of the Average American Household*

- $50,000-a-year gross income
- 2,225 square feet today's average-size house (twice the size of 40 years ago)
- Average U.S. household spends $37,000 per year
- 75% of the $37,000 is spent on necessities (housing, cars, medical and food)
- 25% of the $37,000 ($9,250 per year or $770 per month) is disposable income

*from U.S. Labor Department for year 2000

What this illustration shows is that after the family pays the monthly fixed expenses, such as car loans, mortgages, food, and doctor's visits, that leaves about $9,250 a year for Mom, Dad, and the kids to spend.

What do they buy? Mostly household products and services.

Now, think about this—we've already established that households contain equity, just as houses do, correct? And we just established that the average family spends $9,250 on household products and services each year. Which means each household in America contains $9,250 of annual, renewable equity just waiting to be tapped into.

Average Amount Spent on Household Gold™ in U.S.

etc.

Why Let Others Profit from Your Retail Estate?

Now, when you go to a store to buy your $9,250 of household essentials, you're voluntarily giving someone else permission to tap into your household equity, aren't you? But with the proper positioning, YOU can tap into the equity in your own household, PLUS you can tap into the equity in hundreds of millions of other households all over the world! That's the power of Household Gold!

When you consider there are 118 MILLION households in America alone—well, multiply 118 million households by $9,250 per household, and you come up with this mind-blowing statistic: Americans spend $1,091,500,000,000 (that's **$1.1 TRILLION,** in case you missed it) EACH YEAR on Household Gold products and services.

$1.1 Trillion Opportunity

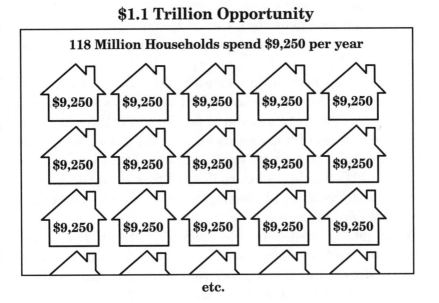

118 Million Households spend $9,250 per year

etc.

Isn't It Time You Mined This Trillion Dollar Opportunity?

We hear the word "billion" being tossed around so much these days that it's hard to comprehend how much a billion dollars really is, so allow me to put things into perspective for you. A billion is a thousand million. A trillion is a thousand billion!

The American economy totals somewhere around $10 trillion a year. *Which means that more than 10% of America's $10 trillion-a-year economy is being spent on Household Gold.*

And that's in just one year! And in just one country!

Wow!

The richest gold or diamond mine in the world doesn't produce anywhere near that kind of revenue. In effect, every household is a goldmine of equity just waiting for you to stake your claim!

Now are you beginning to see the potential of Household Gold? This is what Household Gold is all about—a system whereby you can stake a claim to trillions of dollars in Retail Estate in millions of households all over the globe. Best of all, only a handful of people are even aware that they're sitting on a Household Goldmine. They're like the farmer in the Acres of Diamonds story—they're chasing after diamonds when their own homes are littered with gold.

Your job is make people aware of their Household Goldmines and to help them get started mining their Anyway Money. In exchange for your help, you can receive a percentage of the household essentials that they buy each and every month. Is that a win/win, or what?

Be a Friend of the Trends

Virtually every household product or service can be mined for stealth wealth, but there are two mega-trends that are creating two especially rich veins of Household Gold. The mega-trends I'm talking about are the aging population and the trend toward poor eating habits, which, in turn, leads to weight gain and poor health.

These two mega-trends haven't been lost on consumer giant Proctor & Gamble, which is positioning itself for the future by going after the health and beauty market in a big way. "For P&G, the future appears to be in how consumers look and feel," reports Bruce Horovitz for *USA Today*.

As a result, P&G is committed to acquiring companies that make well-known health-and-beauty brands. Among their recent acquisitions are the Vidal Sassoon, Pantene, and Clairol hair care lines, as well as Noxzema, Cover Girl, and Max Factor beauty lines. P&G is also looking into buying pharmaceutical and/or nutritional supplement manufacturers.

What does P&G's appetite for health and beauty companies mean for you? Simply this. When the biggest consumer products company in the world starts spending billions to buy health and beauty brands, they're sending a message, loud and clear. And the message is this: Although every single product in your home contains stealth wealth, *health and beauty products are destined to become THE dominant product categories in the coming decades.*

Let's take a quick look at the facts that back up these two product-producing mega-trends.

Beauty Products Forecast

People are living longer and families are having fewer children, which is why every major industrial nation, including Japan and all of Western Europe, is adjusting to an aging population. Because of the huge Baby Boom population, the U.S. is leading the way into a "gray new world," as 10,000 Americans turn 50 every single day. Within 30 years, one in five Americans—70 million people—will be 65 or older.

What does this mean for household essentials? First of all, it means a steadily-growing market for beauty products, both domestically and abroad. As populations age, both men and women will be buying age-fighting skin products, such as moisturizers... sunscreens... wrinkle reducers... cleansers... masks... and body lotions. Customized cosmetics and teeth-whitening products will be in big demand, as well as shampoo products that color and thicken as they clean.

Health and Wellness Products Forecast

People have more health challenges as they age, which is bad news for hundreds of millions of soon-to-be seniors but good news for the companies that make and distribute health and wellness products. Obviously, pharmaceutical companies will benefit greatly from a graying world. Statistics show that people 65 and over spend nearly four times as much on keeping healthy as do people under 65.

We're all thankful to be living in an age when modern medicine can cure so many of our diseases. But let's face it, the only thing better than curing a disease with modern pharmaceuticals is not getting the disease in the first place! How do you do that? By supplementing your diet with vitamins and minerals. When you take "nutraceuticals" (a newly-coined word for natural, food-based supplements), you can help protect your body from many preventable diseases, including the three major killers—heart disease, cancer, and strokes.

For example, several huge drug companies sell prescription drugs that lower cholesterol. These drugs help prevent heart attacks, but, as you know, prescription drugs are *very expensive* (and very profitable for drug companies). But scores of studies indicate that diets heavy in certain fruits and vegetables and low in fats are just as effective in lowering cholesterol as prescription drugs. Which means that the number of deaths from heart disease (700,000 people each year in the U.S. alone) could be greatly reduced if people gave up junk food and ate more fresh fruits and vegetables.

But let's get real—people aren't going to start growing their own herb gardens and eating steamed spinach for breakfast. Most people, especially Americans, like their food fast and fat, and that fact isn't going to change. Truth is, most people will not give up pizza and soft drinks in favor of tofu and soy milk. *But most people WILL supplement their diets with disease-preventing nutraceuticals.*

Big Business—and Getting Bigger!

How big is the health and wellness industry? In 2000, North Americans spent $70 billion on nutraceuticals and vitamins. World-renowned economist and bestselling author, Paul Pilzer, predicts the wellness industry will grow from $70 billion to $1 trillion by 2010! Just think—in the coming decade, the U.S. will be spending $1 trillion supplementing their diets with the old standbys, vitamins and minerals, but also with research-based nutraceuticals designed to maximize our physical well being. Here are just a few of the nutraceuticals that are destined to become household essentials in the coming months and years: nutritional shakes and bars... energy maximizers... immune system enhancers...plaque reducers... bone strengtheners... human growth hormones... fiber-rich digesters... memory joggers... muscle toners... and joint pain relievers, all washed down by daily mega-doses of filtered water.

In addition, nutraceutical-enriched meal replacement bars and all-natural and totally safe appetite suppressors will enable millions of Americans to lose unwanted pounds and then maintain their ideal weight.

Pay Now, or Pay Later

Maybe you're one of those people who think that eating a balanced diet is all that people need to stay healthy. Maybe you're one of those skeptics who says you'd rather place your faith in your family doctor rather than in some kooky nutra-whatever. Fine. That's your choice. But consider this. In 2002, there were 100 million visits to doctors offices for cold and flu symptoms. Doctors prescribed antibiotics for 33% of those visits—*despite the fact that colds are caused by a virus and antibiotics don't work on viruses!*

Which scenario makes more sense to you?

To catch a cold and spend money at a doctor's office only to be prescribed an expensive pharmaceutical that doesn't do anything to relieve your discomfort or cure your illness?

Or, to supplement your diet with nutraceuticals that strengthen your immune system so that you avoid catching the cold in the first place?

The answer is obvious, isn't it.

Once again, you need to see the obvious.

For when you see the obvious... you can see the future.

Part 2

Out-Smarting the Claim Jumpers

Despite the closing of venerable chains such as Woolworth's and Montgomery Ward, retailing is still the dominant business model for distributing products and services to consumers.

Chapter 4

All Hail, Retail!

When you shop at retail, you're allowing strangers to take money out of YOUR household and put it into THEIR household.

In effect, when you shop at retail, you're voluntarily opening the door to your Household Goldmine and inviting someone else to step inside and mine it.

4

All Hail, Retail!

*Retailing has been described as
selling things which don't come back
to customers who do.*

—Tom Farmer

O kay, so far we've established that your household is chocked full of products rich in stealth wealth, from the detergent in your laundry room to the furniture in your living room to the nutraceuticals on your kitchen counter.

Now, where do you think most people will be getting all of these products stored on the shelves of their laundry room or in their medicine cabinets?

From retailers, of course.

What is this thing we call "retail?" The root word for retail, *tailler*, comes from a French word meaning "to cut up." Over time, the word retail came to mean the sale of goods in small quantities (selling a "cut of cheese" or a "cut of beef" to one customer at a time). Although retailing has been around for centuries, it's still the predominant means for distributing goods and services to consumers.

From Woolworth to Wal-Mart

For most of recorded history, retailing was a mom and pop enterprise. Until the late 1800s, pushcarts and small storefronts dominated the retailing sector. Then, in 1879, F.W. Woolworth developed a discount retailing concept he called the "five and ten cent" store. Retailing has never been the same. Here's the fascinating story of a legendary entrepreneur who nickeled and dimed his way to a fortune.

In the late 1870s, retail stores in the Midwest came up with a new tactic to lure people into their stores—the five-cent table. Retailers gathered up all of their surplus merchandise and placed it on the five-cent table. Shoppers gobbled up the items and stayed to buy other goods at full price. As a result, the store owner got rid of old merchandise that wasn't moving and increased sales throughout the rest of the store.

Twenty-one-year-old Frank Winfield Woolworth, a low-paid clerk at a dry goods store in Middleton, New York, noticed how quickly items on the five-cent table flew out the door. With the backing of friends and family, Woolworth opened his first five- and ten-cent store. It was an immediate success.

If Woolworth had been a typical retailer of his day, the story would have ended there. He would have operated one successful store and become just another prosperous local businessman.

But Woolworth was ambitious and visionary. He figured if his first store was successful in the small town of Lancaster, Pennsylvania, it could be successful anywhere. So, Woolworth made the daring decision to expand his five- and ten-cent concept into stores all across America, making F.W. Woolworth's the original deep-discount retail chain.

By 1916, every town in the U.S. with a population over 8,000 had a Woolworth's, and in January, 1918, Woolworth opened its thousandth store on Fifth Avenue in New York City.

F.W. Woolworth & Co. was the pioneer in discount retailing. Woolworth's Department Stores survived into the mid-1990s, when the company was forced to close its remaining 400 stores because the population had shifted from downtowns, where most Woolworth's were located, to the suburbs, where a fast-growing retailer called Wal-Mart was rapidly becoming the dominant discount chain, just as Woolworth's had in the first half of the 20th century.

Retail Is Still the King

Retailing has gone through lots of changes since F.W. Woolworth opened his one thousandth store almost 90 years ago. Despite the closing of venerable chains such as Woolworth's and Montgomery Ward, retailing is still the dominant business model for distributing products and services to consumers. When all is said and done, retailing is hot, healthy—and here to stay.

Here are some eye-opening statistics that verify the robust health of retailing.

- Retail sales account for $7 TRILLION worldwide each year.
- Retail is responsible for about 25% of the gross domestic product in six major countries—the U.S., Japan, Germany, the United Kingdom, France, and Italy.

• In China, retailing accounts for 36% of the country's annual revenue, while in India, that figure is a startling 47%.

As for employment in the retail sector, China leads the world with nearly 50 million people in retail. India is second, with 33 million employed in retail, while the U.S. is third with 23 million employees in 2.5 million retail businesses (although the U.S. leads the world in the percentage of people employed in retail, as almost 20% of all U.S. jobs are in the retail sector).

Yes, retail, like every industry in the world, has undergone dramatic changes in the last 100 years, evolving from one-person pushcarts on busy street corners to millions of websites in cyberspace. But no matter what form retail takes, it's still alive and well and represents a huge portion of the world economy.

You May Own Your House—but Who Owns Your Household?

Now, let's take a moment to review the key facts we've discussed thus far.

We've established that retail is a $7 trillion-a-year industry worldwide.

We've established that the average family's biggest asset *by far* is the equity in their homes.

And we've established that households have equity, just as houses do.

You likely own your own house.

But who owns your household?!!!

Think about it. As a homeowner, **you're benefiting financially from your real estate** holdings, that is, the equity in your house or condominium. But have you ever wondered **who's benefiting from your Retail Estate,** that is, the equity of the products and services INSIDE your house?

It's the retailers, that's who!

When you spend your money at a retailer, whether it's located in a mall or online... whether it's a ritzy boutique or a rag-tag factory outlet... you're allowing that retailer to tap into your household equity.

Think about it—when you shop at retail, you're allowing strangers to take money out of *your* household and put it into *their* households. When you shop at retail, you're voluntarily opening the door to your Household Goldmine and inviting someone else to step inside and mine it.

What are you doing? You wouldn't invite a banker into your home to mine the equity in your house, would you? Of course not. So why are you inviting retailers in to mine the equity in your household? It's crazy!

Whoa, people—you're missing the obvious! It's obvious that the equity INSIDE your house is an opportunity to create wealth or retail stores wouldn't be so eager to have you buy your household essentials from them, now would they? I mean, it doesn't get any more obvious than that, folks!

But instead of seizing the opportunity to mine the gold in your Household Goldmine for yourself, you give that opportunity away to someone else. Huh? Can't you see the obvious? Can't you see that YOU should be mining your Household Goldmine, not a retailer you likely don't know or care about?

The simple truth is, while the equity in your house is making a modest amount of money for you and your family, *the equity in your household is making a handful of strangers ridiculously rich!*

Let's turn the page to discover who is getting richer than King Midas mining your Household Gold... *right from under your nose!*

Chapter 5

The Wal-Marting of the World!

You wouldn't think of driving to Wal-Mart to ask them to gobble up the equity in your house, would you? That's insane—no one in his right mind would do such a thing.

Yet, when it's time to buy household supplies and services, millions of people jump into their cars and head to the nearest Wal-Mart so that the Walton family can mine the equity in their Household Goldmine.

Isn't it time you saw the obvious and pushed Wal-Mart and the other retailers out of your goldmine?

5

The Wal-Marting of the World!

I kept saying, "Sam, we're making a good living. Why go out? Why expand so much more? The stores are getting farther and farther away." After the 17th store, though, I realized there wasn't going to be any stopping it.

—Helen Walton
wife of Sam Walton, founder of Wal-Mart

Y ou knew Wal-Mart was a big company. But I bet you didn't know HOW BIG—or how fast it's still growing!

The facts tell the tale of the Wal-Mart whale.

Every week, nearly 100 million shoppers roam the aisles of a Wal-Mart—eight times the number of people that all of the U.S. airlines *combined* fly each week. Wal-Mart's sales on one day in 2002—$1.42 billion—was larger than the annual gross domestic product of 36 countries. With sales of $240 BILLION in 2002, the company is the biggest revenue producer in the world—far surpassing perennial leaders General Motors and Exxon Mobil.

Wal-Mart is also the biggest private employer in the world, employing 1.4 million people. In fact, there are more Wal-Mart people in uniform than the U.S. Army. The company maintains a fleet of 20 jets to help keep top management in touch with the 3,600 domestic stores and 1,200 foreign stores in nine countries from Brazil to China.

Still not convinced Wal-Mart rules the retail world? Check this out. Wal-Mart is the world's largest seller of videos and DVDs, making it a bigger revenue generator for Hollywood than movie theaters.

In addition, Wal-Mart is the biggest distribution channel for Disney, Proctor and Gamble, Kraft, Revlon, Campbell's Soup, and Gillette, as well as the country's biggest seller of groceries... toys... diamonds... CDs... clothing... dog food... detergent... jewelry... sporting goods...videogames... socks... bedding... and toothpaste, not to mention the biggest film developer, optician, energy consumer, and real estate developer.

Wait—there's more! Wal-Mart sells gas... delivers flowers... books vacations... offers its own Internet access ... and is experimenting with selling used cars. In fact, rumors abound that Wal-Mart headquarters in Bentonville, Arkansas, is talking with South Korean automakers about building a Wal-Mart line of cars and trucks!

With these kinds of numbers, you'd think that Wal-Mart's growth would be tapering off. You'd be wrong. In 1992, when founder Sam Walton died, the company was 20% of its size today, and the company plans to speed up growth in the coming decade.

"Could we be two times bigger?" asks CEO Lee Scott. *"Sure. Could we be three times larger? I think so."*

Scott isn't just blowing hot air. The company plans to grow 15% a year by adding at least one new store every day for the next 10 years. Currently, Wal-Mart owns 8% of U.S. retail sales, and at its current growth rate, by 2010, Wal-Mart will reach $1 trillion in annual sales and employ 2.2 million people (it's already the biggest employer in 21 states, employing 1 of every 123 U.S. workers and 1 of every 20 retail employees). Turn this over in your mind—when Wal-Mart reaches $1 trillion in annual sales in a few years, it will control 10% of the $10 trillion-a-year U.S. economy. *Whew!*

Why Give the King of Retailers the Keys to Your Goldmine?

Now, before I continue, I want to make it clear that I'm not criticizing Sam Walton and his family, or even Wal-Mart, for that matter, for their tremendous success. In fact, I applaud them. The story of Wal-Mart is one of the great entrepreneurial success stories in the history of business. They're the biggest and the best at what they do.

But what Wal-Mart does is profit from mining other people's Household Goldmines. Wal-Mart is to retailing what McDonald's is to fast food—it's more than a business. It's an icon. And what the Wal-Mart icon represents to me is the absurdity of people inviting a retail store to mine the equity in their Retail Estate.

I mean, I think it's ironic that people volunteer to allow even a small retailer to mine their Household Gold, much less a behemoth like Wal-Mart. It's not like Wal-Mart and the Waltons need more money. (But I guarantee you, the vast majority of people who shop there DO need more money, big time!)

I'm not criticizing Wal-Mart or any other retailer for taking what people give them. I'm just amazed that more people don't jump aboard the Household Gold train and keep more money in their own households, instead of giving it away to retailers.

Who's Getting Rich from Wal-Mart?

So, if Wal-Mart is destined to become the world's first trillion-dollar-a-year company, who's getting rich from their incredible success? Well, it's certainly not the rank-and-file employees. The median income of a Wal-Mart employee is $12,000 a year, less than half of the national average. It's not even the nearly 5,000 store managers, who average between $40,000 and $50,000 a year.

As is the usual case, the big money is made by the bigwigs. Who are they? The regional managers, who make upwards of $250,000... the senior-level managers, who can earn into the millions each year... and, last but not least, the big stockholders, led by the five heirs of founder Sam Walton.

Before Walton died, he set up a family partnership, Walton Enterprises, which controls 38% of Wal-Mart's stock. Walton's widow, Helen, and his four children own the shares equally. What does that translate to in dollar figures? *About $20 billion each,* give or take a few hundred million here or there.

Because of the 38% ownership position, each of Sam Walton's five heirs is tied for fourth place on *Forbes* magazine's 2003 list of the world's 500 richest people. Truth is, if father Sam were still alive, he'd be worth at least $100 billion, which would be twice the worth of Bill Gates, who is currently holding the title of "Richest Person in the World."

To give you some idea of the Walton family's net worth, the five heirs voted to sell 16 million shares of their stock in order to raise money for a family charity. The sale raised $800 million dollars for charity. How much of a dent did the sale of 16 million shares put in the net worth of the Waltons? *Less than 1%!* Now, that's what I would call financial independence, with a capital INDEPENDENCE!

The Moral of the Story

So, you're probably thinking, "The Walton family is rich. Big whoop! What has that got to do with me?"

Plenty.

Two questions readily come to mind concerning the wealth of the Walton family. One, have you stopped to think about HOW the Walton's got so rich? And two, since the Walton's are already ridiculously rich, WHY do people go out of their way to make them even richer? Let's tackle these two questions one at a time.

First, how did the Walton's get so rich? By doing what the merchants did back in the Gold Rush days—by distributing essential household products and services to an eager and growing market.

As I said in the beginning of this book, the distribution of household essentials isn't a glamorous, get-rich-quick enterprise. It's a lot more glamorous and a lot quicker to strike gold or win the lottery.

But Sam Walton understood the potential of Household Gold and the wisdom of smart-and-steady efforts, and in the 30 years from 1962 to 1992, he distributed enough products through his Wal-Mart chain of stores to become the world's richest man.

Is mining for Household Gold quick and easy? No.

Is it proven and profitable? Yes! Yes! Yes!

Who Would You Rather Make Richer? The Walton Family? Or Your Family?

Now it's time to answer the second question: "WHY do people go out of their way to make the Walton family even richer?" People will tell you they shop at Wal-Mart to "save" money. But as Dr. Bill Quain points out in his classic book *Pro-sumer Power!*, when someone buys a $10 product at 40% discount, they don't "save" $4. *They spend* $6!

Yes, they may have spent less by buying at Wal-Mart. But the fact remains, when someone buys a product for $6 at Wal-Mart, the consumer is $6 poorer, whereas Wal-Mart is $6 richer. In other words, Wal-Mart's INCOME depends on your OUT-GO. And when that happens, the Walton family gets richer, while your family gets poorer.

Look, when you run to Wal-Mart to spend your hard-earned money, you're enabling them to own your household, isn't that true?

Yes, you may own your house.

But Wal-Mart owns your household!

And Wal-Mart owns the households of your family members.

And Wal-Mart owns the households of your friends.

And Wal-Mart owns the households of the friends of your friends.

Truth is, the insatiable Wal-Mart whale keeps swallowing up more and more households at an alarming rate. What's sad is that people are volunteering to line up at the front doors of the world's Wal-Marts for the privilege of having their Household Goldmines plundered by the Wal-Mart whale.

What's wrong with this picture?

What's Wrong with This Picture—and How to Make It Right!

What's wrong is that consumers are overlooking the obvious (just as the miners during the Gold Rush did), while *Wal-Mart and thousands of other retailers are seeing the obvious.* And what's obvious is that households are goldmines because they contain equity, just as houses do.

Now, you wouldn't think of driving to Wal-Mart to ask them to gobble up the equity in your house, would you? That's insane—no one in his right mind would do such a thing.

Yet, when it's time to buy household supplies and services, millions of people jump into their cars and head to the nearest Wal-Mart so that the Walton family can mine the equity in their Household Goldmine.

Isn't it time you saw the obvious and pushed Wal-Mart and the other retailers out of your goldmine?

Don't you get it?—retailers are like claim jumpers back in the Gold Rush days, and you have every legal right to take back your claim.

You set up your household, didn't you?

You're legally and morally entitled to the equity in your household, aren't you?

It's time to reclaim your Household Goldmine for yourself and your family. It's time to take a stand and kick those retailing claim jumpers off your land! The government gave you the right to mine your own Household Goldmine, and, by golly, mine it you will.

So, grab a pick ax and a shovel, and follow me to the next two chapters as I show you how to convert household expenses into household income—and own your own life in the process.

Chapter 6

Household Gold: Your Own Wal-Mart Without the Walls

Household Gold is like owning your own Wal-Mart without the walls—you get all of the benefits of owning a Wal-Mart without the burden of billions of dollars in overhead!

And it's like owning your own Proctor & Gamble without the gamble—you get all the benefits of partnering with a consumer products supplier without taking the gamble of getting laid off or fired.

6

Household Gold: Your Own Wal-Mart Without the Walls

Waste neither time nor money, but make the best of both.

—Benjamin Franklin

If Wal-Mart is so profitable, why aren't more people copying their business model? Because the cost of entry is astronomical, that's why. Wal-Mart will soon sell $300 billion worth of merchandise per year. *But it costs the company $291 billion to make those sales!*

Yes, Wal-Mart is huge. And growing. But so is their overhead. In order to distribute products and services, Wal-Mart corporate has to purchase land... build airplane-hanger-size stores... stock the stores with merchandise from 30,000 vendors... pay the salaries and medical insurance for more than a million workers... build, stock, and operate dozens of city-size regional warehouses... and support newspaper and TV ads in hundreds of cities around the world.

No one has the money to compete with Wal-Mart on their terms. (K-Mart tried, and as I write this, they're still tied up in bankruptcy court). But what if *you could own a Wal-Mart without the walls?*

In other words, what if you could facilitate the distribution of products and services like Wal-Mart does without having to shoulder the huge overhead expenses— now, that would be a concept worth considering, wouldn't it?

You Can Do Almost Anything a Retailer Can Do— Only Better!

Remember—my purpose in writing this book is to teach you the benefits of mining Household Gold instead of allowing retailers to mine it. So, it stands to reason that the first thing you have to do is kick the retailers out of your Household Goldmine so that you can mine the equity instead of them, right? Right!

So, follow along as I spin a scenario whereby you remove the retailers from the product distribution train, enabling YOU, not someone else, to mine your Household Gold. Here we go.

Have you ever thought about what a retailer really does? Most people would answer that retailers sell stuff. Truth be told, most clerks in retail stores don't know the first thing about selling. More often than not, when you go into a retail store to buy household essentials, you've already *sold yourself!* You know what you want. You go to retailers because they can *supply you* with the goods and services you need, not because you need a clerk to sell you something.

So, in effect, retailers are middlemen between the manufacturers and you. Think of middlemen as claim jumpers who are profiting from the gold in your mine. You want them out of the picture so that you can earn the profits instead of them.

Now, what if you could deal directly with a supplier or manufacturer, instead of having to drive to a retailer (or connect to them online) to buy your household essentials? Would that be a good thing? Of course it would.

And, what if you had an arrangement with a supplier whereby they would warehouse all of the products and just ship them to you and your customers on an as-needed basis? Would that be a good thing? Of course it would.

And, what if the supplier gave you discounts and rebates on all of the products you purchased from them? Would that be a good thing? Of course it would.

And, what if the supplier compensated you for sharing the Household Gold concept with others by paying you commissions and bonuses on all of the products and services purchased by the other households? Would that be a good thing? Of course it would.

Well, the good thing I've just described is an overview of how the Household Gold concept works. Household Gold is like owning your own Wal-Mart without the walls—you get all of the benefits of owning a Wal-Mart without the burden of billions of dollars in overhead! And it's like owning your own Proctor & Gamble without the gamble—you get all the benefits of partnering with a consumer products supplier without taking the gamble of getting laid off or fired.

Would that be a good thing? Of course it would!

Anyway Money, Not Additional Money

Now, the great thing about mining Household Gold is that it's based on Anyway Money, as opposed to Additional Money. Many of the household products and services that make up your Retail Estate are consumables, which means they

MUST be replenished on a regular basis. Because much of your Household Gold is based on necessities, you have to buy them with Anyway Money. Literally hundreds of household essentials aren't optional—they're necessities!

Cleaning products aren't optional—they're necessities!

Health and beauty products aren't optional—they're necessities!

Nutritional supplements aren't optional in today's fast-food world—they're necessities!

The list of necessities goes on and on.

Out of necessity, every household has to spend hundreds, if not thousands, of dollars on a weekly and monthly basis just to keep their consumables replenished. Which means that the richest veins in your Household Goldmine are the products and services that you have to spend money on *anyway*.

Unlike most traditional businesses that require lots of Additional Money before the owner can start making profits, Household Gold is based almost entirely on Anyway Money. For example, suppose you wanted to open a retail store. To reduce your risk, you'd likely do what many business owners are doing today, and you'd buy into a franchise. Just look at all the Additional Money you'd have to come up with before you sold your first product to your first customer. You'd have pay a franchising fee... lease space for your store... stock the shelves with inventory... advertise your new business... and pay employees.

When you tally up all your upfront expenses, the Additional Money you'd need to own and operate your new franchise could run into the hundreds of thousands of dollars! Whew!—that's a lot of Additional Money to come up with, and there's no guarantee your business would be profitable!

Thanks, but no thanks!

With for the Household Gold concept, however, it's just the opposite. Household Gold requires very little Additional Money but is designed to tap into LOTS of Anyway Money. Since household essentials have to be purchased *anyway,* you aren't obligated to dip into your personal savings before you can start mining your Household Goldmine.

That's what makes Household Gold such a great opportunity—the downside is small, while the upside is huge! That's why I call Household Gold your "Wal-Mart without the walls"—you enjoy the benefits of a Wal-Mart without the massive overhead. What could be better than that?

Choose Your Level of Participation

Unlike traditional businesses that require a lot of Additional Money, the Household Gold concept doesn't put you behind the financial eight ball. If you own a franchise, you can't be casual about your business—that is, not if you want to stay in business. Franchisees can't come and go as they please... can't set their own hours... can't cut back on their work schedule when there's a family emergency. Franchisees and traditional business owners MUST work hard six days a week or they could lose their shirt!

With the Household Gold concept, you own your own business—*but the business doesn't own you!* Which means you choose the level of participation that you're comfortable with.

With Household Gold, there are basically three levels of participation you can choose from. The first scenario is the **Cash Back Plan.** You can choose to buy your household essentials directly from the supplier/manufacturer and get cash back by way of discounts and rebates.

The second scenario is the **Cash Flow Plan.** In this plan you create cash flow by building a base of regular retail customers and/or by sharing the Household Gold concept with a few other households, thereby earning commissions and bonuses on the products and services they and their circle of clients buy.

The third and final scenario is the **Cash Cow Plan.** In this plan, you act as a full-time professional referral service, sharing the Household Gold concept with other households... and then teaching and training those households to share the concept with other households... who will also learn to teach and train other households, and so on. As your community of consumers grows, you can earn commissions and bonuses on ALL of their purchases, thereby creating a *cash cow* for you and your family.

How Do You Mine for Household Gold?

Now, if you're like most people, you're more interested in the Cash Flow plan or the Cash Cow plan than the Cash Back Plan. And I don't blame you.

Yes, I'm sure you like discounts and good deals when you shop. But if you're like me, you're more interested in exploring ways to diversify your income stream than in saving a few bucks by buying at discount .

That's the reason I started investing in income properties—I wanted to create a stream of residual income that would keep the cash flowing INTO my household whether I was working or not.

And that's exactly what you're going to learn in the next chapter—how to mine your Household Gold to produce maximum profits.

Just as Sam Walton wasn't content to open just one store, I doubt if you're content mining just one household. So, let's turn the page to see how you can mine not just your own Household Goldmine but a whole host of Household Goldmines all over the world!

Part 3

Mining Your Gold

How big is the Household Gold market? Gargantuan—and growing!

A quick review of key statistics proves my point. Multiply 118 million households by $9,250 of disposable income per household, and you get a figure of $1.1 TRILLION PER YEAR, most of which is spent on household essentials.

Chapter 7

How to Mine Household Gold

By moving YOU from the consumer slot to the supplier's rep slot, you position yourself to take a cut of the profits and MAKE MONEY, as Wal-Mart does, instead of SPENDING MONEY, as typical consumers do.

Positioning yourself as a supplier's rep empowers you to convert household products and services from expenses to income— and to own your own life in the process.

7

How to Mine Household Gold

There is no security on this earth.
There is only opportunity.

—*Gen. Douglas MacArthur*

When your children come home from college and announce that they're switching their majors to "Buzz Studies," don't scold them for watering down their academic load. Instead, praise them for having the wisdom to learn about the most powerful marketing strategy in the world—word-of-mouth marketing.

Word-of-mouth marketing is nothing new. As far back as the 1950s, marketing experts were proclaiming that word-of-mouth was the single most effective method for getting consumers to try new products and services.

But it has only been recently that researchers have tried to measure "buzz." Their conclusion? It's not easy to measure word of mouth, but it *is* easy to gage its effectiveness. Word of mouth is by far the most effective means of marketing. Nothing else is even close.

As proof, two Harvard and Yale associate professors researching the word-of-mouth phenomenon point out that 60% of European consumers said that family or friends had influenced them to buy a new brand, and a personal recommendation is overwhelmingly the biggest influence on what new Websites people visit.

The Purpose of Marketing

Whether the type of marketing is word of mouth... or TV commercials... or newspaper ads, all marketing has the same goal—to build a community of consumers. When I use the word "community," I'm not talking about a local neighborhood or small town. By community, I mean a group of like-minded people with common interests, goals, and values, whether those people live in New York, New York or New Delhi, India.

That's why when we hear phrases like "the Christian community" or "the Hispanic community," we understand that certain groups of people share common beliefs, and, as a result, the members of those groups are more prone to buying certain products and services.

Consumer communities can consist of niche markets numbering in the hundreds—say, Grand Master chess players. Or they can consist of mass markets numbering in the hundreds of millions—such as discount-driven shoppers at Wal-Mart. The purpose of marketing, then, is to identify and build a community of consumers for your products and services. And, as we discovered in the opening of this chapter, the best way to do that is through word-of-mouth marketing.

Where Do You Fit in?

So, where do you fit into all of this talk of markets and marketing and Retail Estate? Let me connect the dots for you. In order for you to turn the products and services in your household into Household Gold, first you position yourself as a supplier's rep in the product distribution chain, and then you build a community of consumers (like-minded people with common interests, goals, and values) using word-of-mouth marketing.

Whew—that's a mouthful! But the process of converting retail transactions that *take* your money into Retail Estate that *makes* you money is not as complicated as you might think. What the Household Gold concept boils down to is this: In order to convert your household products from *costing* money to *creating* money, you simply switch from being a consumer at Wal-Mart and other retailers to becoming a supplier's rep for a direct-to-consumer company.

As a supplier's rep, you're an independent business owner compensated with commissions and bonuses, as opposed to an employee compensated with a fixed salary. The upside to being an independent rep is that there's no cap on your income. The bigger you build your community of consumers, the bigger your paycheck.

How Big Is the Market?

How big is the Household Gold Market? Gargantuan—and growing! A quick review of key statistics proves my point.

The average American household has $9,250 of disposable income to spend each year ($770 per month), most of which is spent on household essentials.

Average Amount Spent on Household Gold™ in U.S.

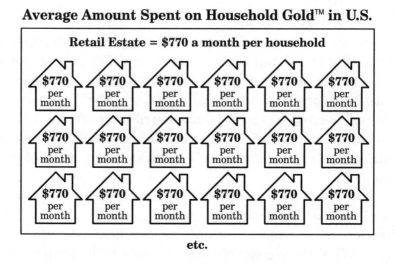

Retail Estate = $770 a month per household

etc.

When you consider there are 118 MILLION households in America alone—well, multiply 118 million households by $9,250 per household, and you come up with this mind-blowing statistic: Americans spend more than **$1 TRILLION EACH YEAR** on Household Gold products and services.

$1.1 Trillion Opportunity

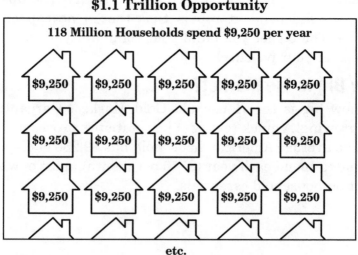

118 Million Households spend $9,250 per year

etc.

Just think, as a supplier's rep, you can position yourself to earn a percentage of an annual TRILLION-DOLLAR MARKET that grows bigger by the year—and that's just the U.S. market.

Worldwide, consumers spend $7 TRILLION EACH YEAR on household products and services. As a supplier's rep, you have no limits on your territory, which means you could earn bonuses and commissions on a multi-trillion-dollar market in dozens of countries around the world! This is the market that the Wal-Mart whale is feeding on, and it's the main reason that Household Gold is a *golden opportunity* if there ever was one!

How Wal-Mart's Product Distribution Chain Works

To better understand your role as a supplier's rep, let's take a moment to describe Wal-Mart's product distribution chain. In a nutshell, here's how products and services are converted to profits in the Wal-Mart model.

First of all, a supplier rep for a supplier/manufacturer (Proctor & Gamble, for example) meets with a Wal-Mart buyer. The supplier rep's job is to negotiate the highest possible price that Wal-Mart will pay for a particular item. Once Wal-Mart purchases that item for say, $10, it's shipped to a Wal-Mart store, where it's marked up 15% above Wal-Mart's cost of $10 (15% of $10 = $1.50), which calculates to the final selling price of $11.50. The item then sits on a shelf at Wal-Mart until a consumer, such as you, purchases it. After paying all of the overhead and expenses, Wal-Mart aims to net 3% of the $1.50 markup, or 4.5 cents.

A flow chart of Wal-Mart's product distribution model looks like this:

Wal-Mart's Product Distribution Chain

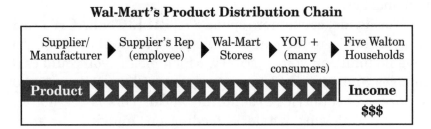

As you study the illustration above, ask yourself who benefits the most financially in the Wal-Mart product distribution chain. Pretty obvious that the big winners are the Wal-Mart Corporation and the households of the five Walton heirs.

Wouldn't you just LOVE to be in Wal-Mart's position and collect a percentage of the $7 trillion that consumers are spending annually on Retail Estate? How would you like to switch places with the Waltons? How would you like to be on the *getting end* of the retail equation instead of the *giving end*?

You can, you know.

How? By switching places on the product distribution/profit chain. In fact, with a simple adjustment of your buying habits, you can cut the Waltons right out of the distribution chain and insert yourself in their place.

Attention all Wal-Mart shoppers! If you're more interested in getting richer by making money from Retail Estate than in getting poorer by spending money at retail stores, then you need to pay special attention to the information you're about to read!

Removing the Wal-Mart Link from the Distribution Chain

We've seen what the Wal-Mart product distribution chain looks like. Now let's take a look at the Household Gold product distribution chain. In the Household Gold chain, you move yourself from the consumer position to the supplier rep position. But instead of being employed by Wal-Mart or the supplier, you operate your own independent business and PARTNER with the supplier. As a result, YOU are positioned to earn the profits, instead of Wal-Mart.

Your Household Gold™
Product Distribution Chain

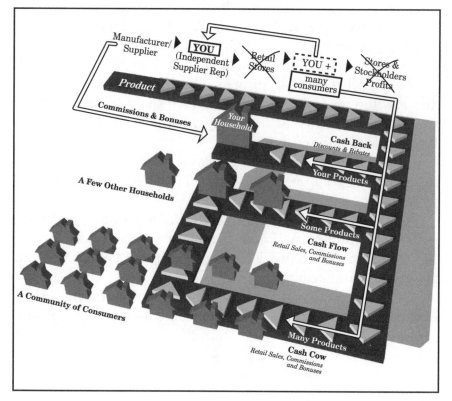

By moving YOU from the consumer slot to the supplier's rep slot, you position yourself to take a cut of the profits and MAKE MONEY, as Wal-Mart does, instead of SPENDING MONEY, as typical consumers do.

This one simple move from the consumer slot to the supplier slot is the key to your tapping into the equity hidden in your Retail Estate. Positioning yourself as a supplier's rep empowers you to convert household products and services from expenses to income—and to own your own life in the process.

Want to Be a Miner?... or a Mining Company?

As you can see, mining Household Gold is a pretty simple process. It doesn't require a lot of expensive equipment or an expensive college education. All it requires is an open mind and a willingness to learn the tricks of the trade from successful miners of Household Gold.

That's all it takes—an open mind... a desire to learn... and a willingness to work. If you have those three qualities, you're on your way to sweeping up the gold dust in your Household Goldmine.

It's up to you how much gold you want to mine. You can mine a little gold, or a lot. After all, it's your business and your choice.

You can choose to work a single claim—that is, just your household—and earn discounts and rebates.

You can choose to work locally, mining the households of a few friends and acquaintances.

Or you can choose to become an international corporation, expanding your mining operations into households around the world.

The gold is there, just waiting to be mined. If you aren't going to mine it, someone else will. So, don't you think it's time to get your fair share of... Household Gold?

Chapter 8

Diversify—or Die!

Historically, blue collar jobs have been the least secure because foreign workers will do the same jobs for much less money. But today's hyper-competitive global economy is forcing profit-starved companies to save money by shipping millions of white collar jobs overseas.

As a result, there is no such thing as job security anymore, motivating more and more employees—from assembly line workers to senior managers—to diversify their income streams by mining Household Gold.

8

Diversify—or Die!

*For the small investor, the best advice may be
the oldest: diversify.*

—Alon Brav
Professor of Finance, Duke University

Here's something I got off the Internet that sums up
how globalization is affecting our lives. The scenario you're
about to read is clever and factual. And for millions of
working-age people, it paints a very scary picture of a
megatrend that is becoming all too common:

> Joe Smith started the day early, having set his alarm
> clock (MADE IN JAPAN) for 6:00 a.m. While his
> coffee pot (MADE IN CHINA) was percolating, Joe
> shaved with his electric razor (MADE IN HONG
> KONG). After cooking his breakfast in his electric
> skillet (MADE IN INDIA), he sat down with his

calculator (MADE IN THE PHILIPPINES) to see how much he could spend today. He put on a dress shirt (MADE IN SRI LANKA), suit and tie (MADE IN SINGAPORE), and dress shoes (MADE IN BRAZIL). After setting his watch (MADE IN TAIWAN) to the radio (MADE IN MALAYSIA), he got in his car (MADE IN MEXICO) to continue his year-long search for a job. At the end of another discouraging and fruitless day, Joe decided to relax for a while. He poured himself a glass of wine (MADE IN CHILE) and turned on his TV (MADE IN INDONESIA). And then wondered why he couldn't find a good-paying job... in... AMERICA!

Although Joe Smith is a fictional character, his everyday experience with household products is very real, as is his fruitless search for a good-paying job. Joe has surrounded himself with dozens of products made in countries all over the globe, but he never stopped to think how his buying those products affects the American economy.

That is, he never thought about it until he started looking for a job.

That's when it hit him—in order to buy more cheap imports, America has had to export its most precious product—*jobs*! Unfortunately for Joe, he didn't think about how globalization is impacting the job market in America until *after* he'd already lost his job, instead of before.

Unemployment: Bad—and Destined to Get Worse

Joe isn't the only one looking for a job these days. As I write this, the unemployment rate, according to government statistics, is 6.4%, which calculates to almost 10 million people in a workforce of almost 150 million.

At least that's what the government says.

Truth is, the *real* number of unemployed is closer to 10% or 15 million people (not to mention the millions of Americans who are seriously *underemployed,* a growing trend that we'll talk more about in a moment). What accounts for the discrepancy between the government's fantasy figures and the *real* figures? Garbled government logic.

You see, Washington only counts people as "unemployed" if they're currently receiving unemployment benefits. Government logic goes like this:

If you lose your job but never apply for unemployment, YOU'RE NOT UNEMPLOYED!

If your unemployment benefits expire, YOU'RE NOT UNEMPLOYED!

If you're a college student just entering the workforce and can't find a job, YOU'RE NOT UNEMPLOYED.

If you've given up looking for a job because it's hopeless... or if you've decided to retire early because you can't find a job, YOU'RE NOT UNEMPLOYED!

Result: There are MANY MILLIONS of Americans desperate for work—but the Labor Department refuses to count them! Here are the real totals: Start with the 9.4 million Americans receiving unemployment... add another 4.7 million who never applied for unemployment benefits or whose benefits have run out—that totals 14.1 MILLION unemployed workers in the U.S. today—50% MORE than Washington admits to!

Then add another 4.8 MILLION who have lost their full-time jobs and are forced to accept low-paying, part-time jobs. The final tally is almost 20 MILLION people, or 13% of the workforce, who are either unemployed or seriously underemployed.

One thing you can say about our friend Joe in the opening story—he's got a lot of company!

The Color of Your Collar Doesn't Count Anymore

Traditionally, assembly line workers are hardest hit by globalization. Blue collar workers are always looking over their shoulders, wondering when their job will be farmed out to Mexico or Asia, where the labor is cheap and plentiful.

White collar "knowledge workers," on the other hand, have always thought their specialized education and know how would insulate them from job migration. And that was pretty much the case until the dot.com bomb exploded in the spring of 2000. Since that time, nearly 3 million jobs have been lost, the majority of which are white collar.

Historically, when a recession is over, white collar workers are the first to be hired back.

Not so this time.

"The vast majority of the 2.7 million job losses since the 2001 recession began were the result of permanent changes in the U.S. economy and are not coming back," says a study from a Federal Reserve Bank of New York.

The job losses cut a wide swath across the economy, to include airline pilots... software developers... middle managers... retailers... and telecom workers, to name a few. The result? To make ends meet, pilots are steering taxis and engineers are pouring coffee at Starbucks. And this is just the tip of the iceberg. Forrester Research, a trend-analysis firm, predicts that 3.3 MILLION jobs will be shipped overseas by 2015, and those jobs "are not just assembly-line work but increasingly are white-collar positions."

White Collars Permanently Stained by India Ink

Today, the world shares jobs as well as goods. And as more foreign workers learn English, the more they're claiming high-paying, white-collar jobs that once belonged exclusively to Americans. Everyday, thousands of formerly "secure," high-wage office jobs in customer support... medical analysis... computer programming... claims processing... form filling... order taking—and, yes, even accounting, architecture, and legal work—are being outsourced to foreign countries.

A recent headline in the *Financial Times* tells the tale: "Service industries go global: how high-wage professional jobs are migrating to low-cost countries." The article goes on to say that of the 13 million financial services jobs in the U.S. and Europe, 2 million are forecast to be outsourced to India, Malaysia, and China by 2008.

Today the world is truly a global village and English is the predominant dialect. That's why 250 million Chinese are studying English, a number nearly equivalent to the population of the United States. And when these English-speaking Chinese enter the workforce, they'll have knowledge... they'll have computers...they'll have Internet access... they'll have cell phones... and they'll be willing to work for 1/10 of the going salary in the U.S.

Add to that tens of millions of educated, ambitious, English-speaking people around the globe, and it means banks, brokerages, and law firms will have an ocean of smart, motivated, low-income workers to fish in, instead of a pond of high-salaried Americans.

What would you do if you headed up a giant bank? Pay Americans $60 an hour (plus benefits) to trouble shoot your IT software? Or fire the entire IT department and outsource the work to $6-an-hour code writers in India? If you wanted to keep your stockholders happy (and keep your job), you'd opt for outsourcing to India, wouldn't you?

Oops, Mr. and Mrs. Knowledge Worker—your white collar just got stained with globalization! But unlike previous job loss stains, this stain can't be bleached out by a booming economy. Because this stain is from India ink. And it's permanent.

You Better Be Ready for the Future—Because the Future Is Now!

A word of warning: Don't get lulled into thinking that the migration of white collar jobs is one of those "that-won't-happen-to-my-job-until-I'm-long-retired" type of trends. As you read this, white collar jobs in the U.S. and Europe are heading to Asia faster than a one-way flight on the Concorde.

Proof: U.S. banks saved $8 BILLION in four years by outsourcing data transaction centers to India. Right now there are Manhattan-based corporations whose executives live in the U.S. and their secretaries in India, where secretaries' salaries are five times lower than in New York.

Are there jobs still available in the U.S? Sure. Lots of 'em. Waiters, bank tellers, hospital staff, and security guards are all in demand. But the work is tedious and the pay is low. As for advancement, the best you can hope for is to get promoted from $6 to $10 an hour, but no matter how good you are, the pay will be capped.

Not a pretty picture, is it?

Be Proactive to Build a Better Life Puzzle!

Look, I know you're probably not standing in the unemployment line as you read this, so you may be thinking all of this talk about job losses doesn't apply to you. But when you step back and look at the big picture, job losses is just one piece of the prospects-for-the-future puzzle.

Here are some other pieces of the puzzle, and they aren't any prettier.

- **Puzzle piece:** *Retirement savings are almost nonexistent for most workers.* According to a congressional study, more than 50% of workers between 25 and 64 don't own any retirement savings accounts.
- **Puzzle piece:** *Less than 50% of workers say they're satisfied with their jobs.* According to the Consumer Research Center, job satisfaction among U.S. workers has hit a record low.
- **Puzzle piece:** *America's corporate pension system is facing a perfect storm.* According to *BusinessWeek,* pension plans are underfunded by $350 billion. To compensate, corporations are selling off units that have older employees, who then lose their pension benefits; other companies are declaring bankruptcy, which means the restructured company can legally cut benefits to retirees and employees.
- **Puzzle piece:** *The middle class is barely treading water.* According to *USA Today,* these days two-income families are struggling to "survive the skyrocketing cost of housing, health care, and college while saving for retirement and shouldering growing debt loads."
- **Puzzle piece:** *About 45% of working adults ages 50 to 70 plan to work beyond 65.* According to an AARP survey, most workers are delaying retirement because of savings lost in the stock market and higher health care costs.

Put all the pieces together, and what do you see? You see a portrait of the typical American family, standing in front of their home. The home is in good condition. The lawn is mowed. The kids are smiling. But mom and dad are frowning. Why? Because they know that behind the picket fence their "stable" middle class life is teetering on the brink of disaster.

What about your life? Do any of these puzzle pieces describe a piece of your life?

Are you happy and fulfilled in your job?

Are your household finances in order?

Do you have enough money set aside for retirement?

Do you pay off your credit card balances each month?

Do you have a secure, high-paying job or own your own successful business?

If you answered NO to any of these questions, then it's time to be proactive and take precautions to head off disaster.

Don't Put All Your Eggs in One Basket

If some of the pieces of your life puzzle don't fit in with the Big Picture you've dreamed for yourself and your family, *then you need to take action now,* not after you've been laid off!

Household Gold offers you a way to make sure that you don't have all your income eggs in just one job basket. By mining Household Gold, you can supplement your income anywhere from a few dollars a week... to a few hundred dollars a month... *to a few hundred thousand dollars a year*! And, unlike franchises, the Household Gold concept only requires a few hundred dollars, or less, to get started (as opposed to tens of thousands of dollars—or even hundreds of thousands of dollars—for traditional franchises).

Plus, you don't have to quit your job to start mining Household Gold. The Household Gold concept enables you to diversify your income stream by sharing the concept with others during evenings and weekends, while maintaining your full-time job. That's the beauty of Household Gold—you can mine it part time or full time. You can mine it fast or slow. Or you can mine a little or a lot. It just depends on your needs, your goals, and, of course, your talents and efforts.

Diversify—or Die!

Think about it—why wouldn't people want to diversify their income? We live in an increasingly competitive world, a world where technology is destroying old business models as fast as it creates new ones. Ten years ago, for example, fax machines were selling like hot cakes. Manufacturers and sellers of fax machines were raking in the dough. But today, thanks to the Internet, fax machines are going the way of the typewriter. So, knowing what you know now, if you were a fax machine manufacturer or salesperson in 1990 , wouldn't you want to diversify your income stream? Of course!

Same goes for your job. The time to diversify your income isn't when times are bad or after you've lost your job. The time to diversify is NOW, while you still have a job... while your industry is still alive and kicking, not when it's dead!

With dramatic changes occurring every few years, instead of over decades or centuries, smart people plan for the worst and hope for the best. And a big part of planning for the worst is to diversify your income while you still can!

When Low Tech Beats High Tech

Technology is speeding up the pace of change in our world, no question about it. But that doesn't mean every "low tech" product has lost its value. On the contrary, some age-old products are so perfectly practical that they just can't be replaced.

Like the pencil, for example.

When a leading design magazine asked Doug Chaing, the Director of Design for Lucasfilm, the company that writes and produces the *Star Wars* movies, what invention was most valuable to the 21st century, he replied, "The simplest of tools, the pencil, will help shape the technological growth promised for the 21st century... [because] the pencil contains the capacity to create, communicate, record, transfer, and structure ideas. Readily available and easily acquired, it's indispensable."

When you think about it, the low-tech pencil has advantages the hi-tech Internet can never emulate. Pencils are cheap. Small. Portable. And always on. And, unlike a computer, if a pencil breaks, you just sharpen it and get back to the task at hand. So the pencil will always have its place, no matter how hi tech the world becomes.

The same can be said for Household Gold products. We tend to glamorize hi-tech products, like PDAs and Internet-equipped cell phones. But when all is said and done, people can live without their hi-tech gizmos.

But you wouldn't even consider trying to live without pure water, would you? Or cleaning supplies? Or health and wellness products? Or shampoo? Or furniture? Or the hundreds of other household products sitting on your counter tops or stored in your cabinets? NO WAY!

Low Tech Equals High Profits

Well, just as the humble pencil will sketch out the technological breakthroughs of tomorrow, our commonplace household goods and services will continue to fuel the growing global economy—today... tomorrow... and forever.

There will always be a HUGE demand for Household Gold products and services, including the demand in your own household. Each year, millions of people will earn billions of dollars supplying products and services to households all over the world—so why not position yourself to earn some of that Household Gold?

If you agree that in our fast-changing world, smart people are choosing to diversify their income streams, rather than putting all of their income eggs in one basket, then what better way to diversify than to make money on products that every household has to buy on a monthly basis *anyway*?

Diversifying your income just makes good sense, doesn't it?

Likewise, the Household Gold concept just makes good sense, too—as in "dollars and cents!"

So, what are you waiting for?

Make your tomorrows more prosperous and secure by diversifying your income—*today*!

Conclusion

It's obvious that someone is going to mine your Household Goldmine—so it might as well be you!

It's obvious that since you have to spend the money on household essentials anyway, you might as well get your fair share of those sales, rather than a retailer.

So, see the obvious!

Conclusion

The Legend of the Touchstone Scroll

*Too many people are thinking of security
instead of opportunity. They seem more
afraid of life than of death.*

—James F. Byrnes

In ancient times, the royal library in Alexandria, Egypt, was the cradle of recorded civilization, housing nearly a million scrolls of literature, science, philosophy, medicine, geography, and astronomy.

Sadly, during a siege in 640 A.D., the library burned to the ground, and all of the recorded wisdom of the ages went up in smoke. Modern scholars assert that every document was destroyed.

But legend has it that a single, small scroll survived.

Here is the story of the single surviving scroll from the great library of Alexandria.

The Legend of the Touchstone Scroll

While the invaders set fire to each corner of the royal library, an old librarian hid in a narrow alley, watching as the flames licked the sky. Days later, when the once-grand building had been reduced to a smoldering heap, the librarian waded through the rubble, picking at the remains with a stick. Not a scroll remained.

As the heartbroken librarian turned to leave, his foot knocked over a charred chamber pot, revealing a small yellowed scroll, the only remaining document from the entire library of Alexandria. The librarian grabbed the scroll. Brushing the ashes from the scorched label, the librarian read the title: "The Secret of the Touchstone." He glanced around nervously and then scrambled out of the ruins to investigate his find.

As the librarian eagerly read the scroll, the secret of the touchstone was revealed. The touchstone was a small pebble with magical powers. Any material that came into contact with the touchstone would be instantly turned into gold!

The scroll explained that the magical touchstone looked like thousands of other pebbles littering a high, secluded cliff overlooking a roaring inlet of the Mediterranean Sea. But the secret was this: The real touchstone would feel warm, while ordinary pebbles were cold.

The librarian hurried to the cliff and began his search for the touchstone. He knew he had to have a system for eliminating the ordinary pebbles from the real touchstone, so he devised a plan: Every time he picked up a cold pebble, he would throw it into the sea, thereby narrowing his search for the warm, true touchstone.

The librarian spent his first day from sun up to sun down, picking up cold pebbles and tossing them into the churning sea. He worked methodically, making sure that not a single stone escaped his grasp. Days stretched into weeks as he scoured the cliff in sections, until at last, he had narrowed his search to one small section of rocky terrain.

"It won't be long now," he said to himself as he worked his way across the cliff. "At the most I have two days of work left, perhaps three. Soon the touchstone will be mine!"

He smiled as he picked up yet another pebble and automatically tossed it into the sea—and then collapsed in shock. *That last pebble was warm!*

Moral of the Story

Like the old librarian in the story, we're all creatures of habit. The old librarian had developed such a strong habit of throwing away worthless pebbles that when he finally found the priceless touchstone he'd been looking for, he unthinkingly tossed it into the sea.

So it is with opportunities, as well as touchstones. Unless we pay careful attention, it's easy to ignore an opportunity, especially if it's familiar and right under our noses!

Like the touchstone in the legend, the products and services in your household don't look like they contain hidden wealth-creating powers. If you're like most people, the stuff in your household is so familiar to you that you take it for granted, just as you took for granted that retail stores are the best places to acquire your household essentials.

But that was before you read this book!

Household Gold: Your Touchstone for Wealth Creation

Think of this book as your Touchstone Scroll. By reading this book, you've learned the secret that can transform ordinary household essentials into Household Gold.

You've learned that, unlike most great opportunities, the Household Gold concept doesn't require much Additional Money because it taps into Anyway Money, which is money you have to spend to maintain your household *anyway.*

You've learned that just as real estate has equity, your Retail Estate contains equity, also.

You've learned that the average American family has $9,250 of disposable income to spend each year, most of which is spent on household products and services.

You've learned that almost every single product in your household—mined either separately or collectively—contains enough Household Gold to create a steady stream of income for you and your family.

You've learned that most households are allowing retailers (led by Wal-Mart) to take $7 trillion a year from their Household Goldmines.

You've learned that the Household Gold concept is like owning your own "Wal-Mart without the walls" and that all you have to do to make money from Household Gold is to insert yourself in the product distribution chain in place of the retailers.

And you've learned that with the Household Gold concept, you can earn *cash back...* create *cash flow...* or build a *cash cow,* depending on your own personal dreams, goals, and efforts.

Don't Toss Away Your Touchstone

These are a few of the things you've learned in this book. Now, I recognize that a few people will do as the old librarian in the *Legend of the Touchstone Scroll* did—they will toss this opportunity away without giving it a second thought, for their daily routine will win out over their new-found wisdom.

But I also know that most people will recognize that they've been overlooking the obvious for too many years, namely, that someone is going to mine their Household Goldmine—so they may as well mine it themselves!

It's obvious that since you have to spend the money on household essentials anyway, you might as well get your fair share of those sales, rather than a retailer.

So, see the obvious!

If you, like me, see the obvious, then do your due diligence and learn more about the Household Gold concept. Folks, unlike the touchstone, Household Gold isn't warm—it's hot. And getting hotter by the day.

So, don't be casual and toss the Household Gold concept away. Learn and apply the principles in this book to your household essentials and teach others to do the same. And then watch in amazement as ordinary products and services are magically transformed into... Household Gold!

Why It's Crucial to See the Obvious!

Seeing the obvious is a matter of common sense, not intelligence. Which is why smart people sometimes fail to see the obvious. As a result, they sit on the sidelines while less talented people are making a fortune.

Don't be like the famous people on the next page who out-smarted themselves by turning a blind eye to the obvious. Open your eyes to the obvious, and you'll see the gold in households all over the world, just waiting to be mined by you.

Why It's Crucial to See the Obvious!

Famous People Who Failed to See the Obvious

Radio has no future. Heavier-than-air flying machines are impossible. X-rays will prove to be a hoax.

I have not the smallest molecule of faith in aerial navigation other than ballooning.

William Thomson, Lord Kelvin (1824–1907)
English scientist;
president of the Royal Society

Space travel is utter bilge.

Sir Richard van der Riet Wooley
The Astronomer Royal, 1956

While theoretically and technically television may be feasible, commercially and financially I consider it an impossibility, a development of which we need waste little time dreaming.

Lee DeForest (1873—1961)
American inventor

There is a world market for about five computers.

Thomas J. Watson (1874–1956)
founder and first president, IBM Corporation

The [flying] machines will eventually be fast; they will be used in sport, but they should not be thought of as commercial carriers.

Octave Chanute (1832–1910)
French aviation pioneer

As far as sinking a ship with a bomb is concerned, it just can't be done.

Clark Woodward (1877–1967)
rear admiral, U.S. Navy

That is the biggest fool thing we have ever done... The [atomic] bomb will never go off, and I speak as an expert in explosives.

William Leahy (1875–1959)
admiral, U.S. Navy

Who would want to hear actors talk?

Harry M. Warner (1881–1958)
founder, Warner Bros. Studio (in 1927,
considering the possibility of talking pictures)

They couldn't hit an elephant from this dist—

last words of U.S. general John Sedgwick
(1813–64) at the Battle of Spotsylvania